Skin Deep

A LOVE LETTER TO SELF

BY BHAVIKA JAIN

Dedication~
To everyone who is judged in some or the other
way ~judge them back.

Preface~

As an 11th-grade student, I find myself constantly
engrossed in the world of books, movies, and
television shows, thanks to my binge watching
addiction. There's something different about diving
into a story, where the characters that I read about
come alive and their journeys, it feels like I am
with them. As a teenager whose biggest life
problems are revolved around my curfew timings,
tests scores and school gossip, my love for reading
and binge-watching has not only provided me
more countless hours of entertainment but also
served as a wellspring of inspiration for my own
writing.

In each narrative I immerse myself in, I become a
silent observer, feeling the triumphs and
heartaches of the characters as if they were my
own. Their struggles resonate with me, often
mirroring my own experiences in life. This
connection allows me to explore emotions and
situations from a fresh perspective, prompting me
to ask: How would they handle this? What would
they feel? What would i feel if i were in place of
them?

In crafting this poetry novel, I have endeavored to
channel these reflections into words, writing from
the characters' viewpoints as they navigate their
challenges and dreams. Each poem is a glimpse
into their thoughts and feelings, shaped by my own
understanding and experiences. Through this
process, I have learned that storytelling is not just
about the plot; it's about the emotions that bind us
all together.

I hope that as you read these poems, you can understand my thought process and learn of my inspirations—about the characters who have shaped my thoughts and the experiences along with my understanding as to how I view the world. Maybe you can connect to me, relate to me as I share perspectives on things that I see happening around me as a teenage girl.

Introduction~

As I stand on the cusp of adulthood, I find myself struggling between with the weight of expectations, the desire for acceptance, and my own identity. The poems that you are going to be reading within these pages are inspired by an interconnected idea of my observations of the world around me, the characters I've encountered in stories, and the silent battles that many of us fight daily. My poems reflect the duality of our existence. Heavy words I know! But in this book I aim to question our society.

In this book, you will be able find themes of conformity, acceptance, self-questioning and much more. As you read, I hope for you to absorb every piece with and open-mind so that you can place yourself in these reflections. Consider how they echo your own experiences and emotions. Let them serve as a reminder that you are not alone in your journey.

Through the lens of poetry, we can connect, share, and find solace in the shared human experience.

In the Depths of a Sapphire Soul

Blue is the color that wraps me tight,
A hue that whispers, urging me to take flight.

It's the shade of my sadness, my silent despair,
A reminder that life isn't always fair.

A color of tears that stain my cheek,
A chill that envelops, making me weak.

Blue is the loneliness that echoes in me,
A shadow that lingers, a haunting decree.

It weighs like a rope, heavy and tight,
As I watch others dance in the starry night.

While they laugh and they twirl, I'm lost in my
gloom,
In a world full of color, I feel trapped in a tomb.

It's hard to see past this endless blue,
To find a glimmer of hope that can pull me
through.

Ruins of Innocence

War, the indicator of sorrow and pain,
War brings death and destruction to land.

War is the reason why bombs rain down like drops
of acid,
War leaves nothing but ruins in their wake.
War is the child of woe that leaves nothing to take.

Families torn apart, every home is in tarnishing
flames,
Lives permanently lapsed, permanently stained.
The frightened calls of innocent dying and nailed,
Echo through the night, like raindrops dancing in a
terrain.

Children hold guns in their hands,
Their families left to grieve.
They sleep well, knowing that they will return,
But in what condition is the only things that
haunts them in their dreams

Thousands of lives are lost, there is so much
bloodshed,
In the name of power, even tears go unshed.
When will we learn that war only brings despair?
All that is left to wonder is the path to repair.

The Sovereignty of Strange Strangers

He whispered desires, yet knew not my name,
Hands pressed tight, a grip that felt like chains.
It wasn't the fabric or the way I styled my hair,
For light, darkness exist everywhere.

He left my house like a monster laughing,
I remember when he said 'don't you cry, my
darling'.
So I stopped seeking monsters beneath my own
bed,
When real terrors roamed where the bloody streets
spread.

Labels of shame, they started casting like a net,
But they're blind to the truths that I can't forget.
Whore, slut, you should lay in the grave.
Was it my fault? Did I somehow invite this
charade?

Fractured

I look upon this form of mine,
And see no beauty, no design.

The world's harsh gaze, a judgment clear -
I am not what they wish to see, I fear.

My curves do not align with grace,
My features fail to match their pace.

I fall so short of their ideal,
My very self, I cannot heal.

How can I love what others scorn?
This flesh, these bones, an ugly thorn.

I wish to be what they think is fair,
But my reflection only holds despair.

I see no radiance, no wonder true,
Just flaws that keep me from their view.

Their standards high, my worth so small,
I cannot seem to love myself at all.

Conformity

In a world of mirrors, reflections collide,
Each face a unique canvas, with stories inside.

Yet whispers of "perfect" echo in halls,
Where beauty is measured by rigid stone walls.
Fighting for beauty, they mask their true face,
A heavy foundation, a fragile embrace.

Their laughter, a melody, stifled and shy,
For fear of the judgment that lingers nearby.
They wear their heart cloaked in layers of doubt,
Afraid that their essence might flicker out.

But beneath the facade, a brilliance does glow,
A tapestry woven with colors that flow.
Each soul is a star, unique in its light,
Yet society beckons, "Conform, fit the sight."

With eyes that are critical, and hearts that are cold,
They mold us to fit into boxes of old.
In this harsh landscape, where kindness is rare,
The weight of perfection hangs heavy in air.

So many are lost in the chase for approval,
While the truth of their beauty remains
unapproved.

The Chameleon

In mirrors held by others' hands,
I shift and mold to meet their demands.
A chameleon in a world so cold,
My essence fades, my truth untold.

I wear their masks, each one a guise,
To dance in tune with their hollow lies.
With every change, I lose a part,
A fractured soul, a heavy heart.

Their whispers guide my every move,
In selfishness, I strive to prove.
I am a puppet pulled,
And yet, they tell me to improve.

The world has become so ungrateful.

I trade my dreams for fleeting praises,
In crowded rooms, I lose my ways.
To fit their mold, I bend and break,
A hollow shell for their own sake.

Yet in the quiet, a voice remains,
A whisper soft that still complains.
"Remember who you used to be,
Before the world decided what it wanted you to
be."

Obscurity

In a race where shadows stretch and bend,
The finish line is drawn, but there's no true end.
Each heartbeat quickens, a pulse of despair,
As eyes scan the crowd, searching for care.

They measure success with a ruler of gold,
While the stories of struggle remain untold.
For every late night spent wrestling with doubt,
There's a silence that echoes, a scream without
shout.

I toil in the shadows, a warrior unseen,
Fighting for moments that might never glean.
Each step that I take is a battle, a fight,
Yet all that they see is the fall, not the flight.

I pour out my heart, my sweat and my tears,
But they only remember the echoes of fears.
In the glare of their judgment, I crumble and
break,
While the weight of my effort is lost in their wake.

They cheer for the winners, the flawless, the
bright,
While I linger in corners, consumed by the night.
For every small victory, a mountain I've climbed,
Yet the world's gaze is fixed on the failures I find.

I've wrestled with demons, faced storms in my
mind,
But the light of my struggle is too often blind.
I wish they could see the strength in the try,

The courage it takes just to reach for the sky.

But here in this chaos, where praises are few,
I search for the solace in all that I do.
For in every attempt, there's a story to tell,
Of a heart that keeps beating, despite every fall.

Whim

In the quiet whispers where moments decay,
We rush through our days, lost in dismay.
The small things linger, unnoticed, unseen,
A flower's faint fragrance, a memory, a dream.

Petals unfurl, yet we turn away,
Ignoring the beauty that fades into gray.
The scent of the earth after rain's fleeting sigh,
A reminder of moments we let pass by.

The warmth of the sun on a cold, weary face,
The rustle of leaves, a forgotten embrace.
Each texture, each sound, a ghost of the past,
Yet we hurry along, too busy to last.

The laughter of children, now echoes of pain,
The simple "I love you" lost in the rain.
In the chaos of life, we neglect to perceive,
The magic in moments, the heart that can grieve.

The softness of fabric, the chill of a hand,
The taste of sweet fruit, the grains of fine sand.
Each detail, a shadow, a whisper of loss,
Yet we race past the wonders, not counting the
cost.

So, pause for a moment, let silence unfold,
Breathe in the stillness, let your heart feel cold.
For life's fleeting pleasures are often concealed,
In the small, quiet moments, our senses repealed.

Mirage

In the glass of illusion, a figure stands tall,
Layers of foundation, a shield from it all.

With each stroke applied, a smile takes flight,
Yet inside, a tempest stirs deep in the night.

The shape-shifter glides, bold in its dance,
In vibrant arenas, it seizes each chance.

A jester in motion, yet trapped in the guise,
As it bends to the crowd, it forgets its own eyes.

The silent observer lingers on the fringe,
Wishing for courage yet feeling the cringe.

Draped in the latest, it mimics their cheer,
But inside, a whisper begs, "Will they see me
here?"

The butterfly flutters, bright wings in the fray,
The life of the party yet yearning each day.

With laughter as armor, it flits through the night,
Yet craves deeper bonds, those unguarded sights.

The perfect facade is crafted with care,
A strained, a life beyond compare.
Each snapshot a moment, a curated bliss,
Yet behind every filter, a longing for this.

Beneath all the layers, the masks that they wear,
Are hearts full of struggles, a burden to bear?

They change and adapt, seeking warmth in the
cold,
Yet yearn for acceptance, for stories untold.

In a world full of faces, they search for the real,
To be seen for their truths, to be heard and to feel.

A Silent Witness

In the stillness I stand, a witness to pain,
With eyes wide open yet feeling the strain.
The cries of the voiceless echo in air,
While I remain silent, caught in despair.

I watch as the strong take what's not theirs,
The weak left to tremble, swallowed by cares.
Each act of injustice, a weight on my chest,
A burden of guilt that I cannot rest.

I see the injustice, the struggle, the fight,
Yet my feet are anchored, paralyzed by fright.
The voices of many call out for change,
But I fear the unknown, the chaos, the strange.

The faces of anguish, the tears that they shed,
Haunt me in dreams, fill my heart with dread.
I wish I could stand, take a step to defend,
But the fear of the backlash makes my courage bend.

I ponder my role in this cycle of woe,
Am I just a bystander, too afraid to grow?
The weight of inaction, it gnaws at my soul,
As I wrestle with feelings I cannot control.

Each moment of silence feels like a crime,
As I grapple with guilt, the passage of time.
What if I spoke? What if I dared?
To challenge the system, to show that I cared?

Yet still, I remain, a ghost in the fray,

Watching the struggle, while hope slips away.
The cries for justice, they pierce through the night,
And I'm left with the question: will I join the fight?

In the depths of my heart, I know I must change,
To rise from inaction, to step from the strange.
For the world needs the courage that lies in us all,
To stand against injustice, to answer the call.

Marked Roles

In this world, roles are drawn so clear,
Women nurture, while men persevere.

With tender hands, women cradle the young,
Yet whispers of duty weigh heavy on the tongues.

"Be the light," they insist, "in every home,"
While dreams of their own are left to roam.

Men, the warriors, stoic and strong,
"Work hard, don't cry; it's where you belong."

With shoulders burdened by the weight of the grind,
Emotions suppressed, their true selves confined.

But what of the hearts that yearn to break free?
To redefine love, to just simply be?

Can a mother not dream, or a father not weep?
In a world that insists we play roles so deep?

The Mutes

In a world of hues, where emotions are bound,
I swallow the colors, my silence profound.
Each morning, I rise, a palette of dread,
With watchers who linger, their gaze like a thread.

"Take blue for calm," whispers the voice,
"Yellow for joy, it's your only choice."
But what of the anger that simmers below?
What of the red that longs to explode?

"Green brings you peace," they insist with a smile,
Yet inside I'm restless, it's all just a trial.
The pills are a prison, each shade a disguise,
Hiding the chaos, the truth in my eyes.

The monitors flicker, they capture my sighs,
In shadows I linger, where freedom just dies.
"Orange for passion," they say with a grin,
But passion feels dangerous, a spark from within.

What if I falter, what if I stray?
Would they strip me of color, and turn me to gray?
"Take purple for dreams," they gently implore,
Yet dreams feel like shackles, a life to ignore.

I hear the machines hum, their eyes ever near,
A constant reminder of all that, I fear.
"White is for clarity," they preach with disdain,
But clarity's cold, just a mask for the pain.

In the stillness of night, when the colors retreat,
I'm left with the echoes of a heart that won't beat.

Each pill a reminder of what I can't feel,
A spectrum of safety, a false sense of reality.

So, I sit in this silence, my spirit confined,
A prisoner of colors, with nowhere to find.
In this world of control, where emotions are sold,
I ache for the warmth of a life uncontrolled.

Words of a Sold Identity

In a marketplace bustling, where memories trade,
I sift through the fragments, the choices I've made.

Each moment for sale, a price on the past,
Yet the weight of their worth leaves my heart
overcast.

"Take joy from the summer," they offer with glee,
"Or sorrow from winter, just a memory fee."

But what of the laughter that echoes in me,
Or the pain that has shaped who I'm destined to
be?
I watch as they barter, their lives on display,
Trading pieces of self for acceptance each day.

Yet in the bright lights, I feel so misplaced,
A jigsaw of moments, my truth laid to waste.

"Forget all the failures, embrace what is new,"
They say with a smile, as if that will do.

But the lessons of struggle are etched in my core,
And I'm torn between wanting and longing for
more.

The faces around me, they shimmer and shine,
While I wrestle with choices that blur the divine.

To fit in the mold, to wear their delight,
Yet the thought of erasure keeps me up at night.

"Here's bliss from the past, it's easy to take,"
But what of the heartache, the risks that we take?

With every transaction, my essence feels thin,
As I barter my soul for a place to fit in.

Away

In a room full of faces, I stand on the edge,
A spectator of laughter, a silent pledge.

They dance in their circles, while I drift away,
A ghost in their joy, I silently sway.

With every bright smile, I feel more unseen,
An outsider peering through a fragile screen.

They share in the moments that spark and ignite,
While I watch from a distance, my heart gripped
by fright.

I wear a facade, a mask of pretense,
Yet inside I'm crumbling, a wall of defense.

Their glances are fleeting, their words like a knife,
Each echo a reminder of the struggle for life.

"Just be who you are," they casually say,
But the weight of their judgment keeps my truth at
bay.

I long to belong, to feel warmth in the fray,
Yet I'm lost in the currents, swept further away.

I search for connection, for hands reaching out,
But the silence surrounds me, filled with self-
doubt.

Each laugh that I hear feels like a distant chime,
A reminder that fitting in is a mountain to climb.

Silent Reaper

Oh, Death, you stand with a gaze so profound,
In the quiet of life, where your presence is found.

You wear a cloak woven from tales of the lost,
A figure of silence, yet you carry the cost.
I see how you gather the weary and worn,
With hands that are gentle, yet hearts you have
torn.

What do you seek in the lives that you claim?
Is there solace in endings, or just endless shame?

I wonder of choices that lead to your door,
Do you whisper sweet promises, or leave hearts
sore?

In the stillness of night, when the world holds its
breath,
Do you cradle the souls, or is it merely theft?

You dance in the shadows of every goodbye,
A reminder that all things must one day comply.
Yet in your embrace, there's a truth that feels raw,
The ache of the living, the love that you saw.

What stories you carry, what secrets you keep,
Of dreams left unfinished, of promises deep.

Do you linger in sorrow, or revel in peace?
In the cycle of time, does your grip ever cease?

I long to understand the weight that you bear,

To know if you mourn for the lives that you share.
For in your cold grasp, there's a warmth that I
crave,
A connection to those who once danced, once
braved.

So, tell me, dear Death, as you walk through the
years,
Do you feel the love mingled in all of our tears?
For every farewell, there's a story untold,
A legacy woven in hearts made of gold.

The Uninvited Guest

Poison, a guest in my home, so sly,
With a smile that lingers, a soft, gentle lie.

It wraps around moments, whispers in air,
A presence so subtle, yet heavy with care.
Each day it sits close, a comfort I know,
In laughter it mingles, in silence it grows.

It sips from my spirit, a thief in disguise,
While I dance to its tune, unaware of the ties.
"Just a taste," it insists, "you'll feel so alive,"
Yet beneath that allure, my essence won't thrive.

It promises sweetness, a thrill to behold,
But deep in my veins, it's a story untold.
In gatherings cheerful, it plays the best part,
With charm that entangles, it captures my heart.

Yet as I reach out, I feel its cold grip,
An anchor that pulls me, a slow, silent slip.
It colors my thoughts, turns joy into dread,
With every shared secret, it whispers instead.

"Let go of your burdens, embrace what I give,"
But each fleeting moment, I struggle to live.
In the quiet of night, when the laughter has ceased,
I sense its presence, a hunger unleashed.

It feasts on my dreams, each hope it consumes,
A shadow that looms in the depths of my rooms.
I ponder its power, the hold that it keeps,

As it weaves through my mind, while my spirit
weeps.

"Why do you linger? What do you gain?"
Yet it smiles, unfazed, as I drown in the pain.
With every sweet promise, it crafts a fine thread,
Binding me closer, as I lay in its bed.

Alice in my Wonderland

In a realm where logic bends and sways,
I find myself lost in a wild ballet.

One moment I'm soaring, the sky is my friend,
Then suddenly tripping, the dance takes a bend.

A creature comes rushing, its eyes full of fire,
I stumble and tumble, consumed by desire.

The ground shifts beneath me, a chasm appears,
As I run from the monster, I'm swallowed by fears.

The colors swirl wildly, a canvas in flux,
With landscapes that twist, and my mind in a flux.

I'm racing through fields, then caught in a storm,
Where time loses meaning, and chaos is norm.

I reach for a hand, but it slips through my grasp,
A fleeting connection, like sand in a clasp.

Each turn brings a riddle, a puzzle unspun,
In this realm of the restless, where dreams come
undone.

A voice calls my name, yet it echoes away,
As I chase after shadows that refuse to stay.

What once felt familiar now shifts with a sigh,
In a tapestry woven of truth and of lie.

Here laughter can echo, yet sorrow can creep,

As I dance through the layers, both shallow and
deep.

With each fleeting heartbeat, the story unfolds,
A journey of wonders, both timid and bold.

So, I wander through landscapes, both vivid and
strange,
In a world where the ordinary bends and can
change.

For in this wild dreamscape, where freedom is
found,
I embrace the unpredictability of my dreams that
know no bounds.

Bonfire

Let me tell you a secret, a truth wrapped in flame,
He smelt like bonfire, igniting my name.

With every encounter, the warmth spread so wide,
A flicker of hope, where my fears used to hide.
In his laughter, I found the spark of my dreams,
Each word that he spoke, a chorus of themes.

He lit up the corners where doubt used to dwell,
With a glance, he could weave a magical spell.
I wanted to run, to dance in the heat,
To chase after passions, to rise to my feet.

He taught me to build, to gather the kindling,
To stoke the desire, to set my heart singing.
With every shared moment, the embers grew
bright,
He turned my mundane into radiant light.

The effort I put in, like logs on the fire,
Fueled by the warmth of a newfound desire.
No longer a flicker, I burned with intent,
Each day a new canvas, my spirit unbent.

He showed me the beauty in crafting my tale,
In the flames of my heart, I could never grow pale.
When I felt like ashes, he breathed life anew,
A bonfire of courage, igniting my view.

I reached for the stars, with the fire in my soul,
In a dance of creation, I finally felt whole.

Dark Serenity

In the garden of stillness, a figure stands tall,
With arms wide open, inviting us all.
A gentle caress, a soft, tender sigh,
Whispering promises as the moments pass by.

She dances with grace, a waltz through the years,
Collecting our burdens, our laughter, our tears.
In her embrace, the weary find peace,
As she cradles their dreams, granting sweet
release.

Her touch is a balm, soothing the ache,
A lullaby sung for each heart that will break.
With petals of comfort, she blankets the ground,
While echoes of life in her presence resound.

She beckons the restless, the lost and the brave,
A siren of solace, a shimmering wave.
In twilight's soft glow, she paints the horizon,
A canvas of endings where new paths can brighten.

With every farewell, she whispers a tale,
Of journeys uncharted, where spirits set sail.
In her arms, the weary shed layers of strife,
Finding beauty in silence, in the rhythm of life.

She weaves through the fabric of time's endless
thread,
Embracing the living, honoring the dead.
In the stillness, she promises grace,
A dance of remembrance, a sacred space.

For in her soft glow, we learn to let go,
And cherish the moments that flourish and flow.
In the garden of stillness, where life meets its close,
She only judges us by the seeds that we've sown.

Multiverse

Is there a world beyond this breath?
A realm untouched by life or death?

If the sky stretches wide and free,
What lies beyond its mystery?

I gaze at stars that twinkle bright,
Like diamonds scattered in the night.

Each question floats like clouds that drift,
In shadows deep, my thoughts they lift.

If nothing exists, how vast is this space?
Does it cradle dreams in a silent embrace?

I seek the edges of this endless sea,
Tracing the lines of what's yet to be.

I've chased the whispers of doubt and fear,
Trading my truths for the dreams I hold dear.

Yet here I stand at the void's edge,
Awash in wonder, ready to pledge.

For in this quest, a spark starts to glow,
Illuminating paths I yearn to know.

Is there a sky where the lost can soar?
Or merely silence that beckons for more?

Okay to Not Be Okay?

When I ponder the choice that weighs on my heart,
I offer the answers that keep me apart.
I say it's simple, just let you go,
But how can I sever the ties that still flow?

Each memory lingers, a ghost in my mind,
A tapestry woven yet frayed at the bind.
I wear a brave smile, pretend I'm okay,
While inside, I wrestle with words left to say.

Because the truth is a burden, a weight that I bear,
In the silence, I feel you are always right there.
What can I do with this ache that won't fade?
This longing for moments that never were made?

I recall every glance, each unspoken word,
The feelings unvoiced, yet profoundly heard.
That bond, that connection, which never took
flight,
A flicker of hope lost in the night.

I wish I could silence the thoughts that persist,
But the echoes of you linger, too strong to resist.
So, I stand at this crossroads, unsure of the way,
Caught in the cycle of what I can't say.

For perhaps it's the fear of what might have been,
That keeps me entangled in places I've been.
In the depths of my heart, I know it's not right,
Yet I'm tethered to dreams that dissolve in the
light.

Price of Class

In the marketplace where class is sold,
Where whispers of worth are brazen and bold,
A cacophony rises, a symphony stark,
Where privilege dances, igniting a spark.

Here, the rich wear their crowns made of gold,
While the poor clutch their dreams, frayed and
cold.
With every transaction, a soul's value weighed,
In this bustling bazaar, humanity swayed.

"Step right up!" calls the merchant with glee,
"Buy your status, your place, your decree!
For a taste of respect, a slice of esteem,
You can barter your way into someone's dream."

The laughter of children mixes with cries,
As the scales tip heavy beneath painted skies.
A mother stands weary, her hands worn and tired,
While the elite sip their wine, their privilege
admired.

Oh, Dear Heart! Again?

"Dear heart, why do you linger in this fray?
In the shadows of wealth, do you long for the day?
When kindness is currency, not just a façade,
When the worth of a soul isn't measured by odds?"

Yet the crowd keeps on swirling, the game never
stops,
As the poor watch the wealthy from their
makeshift shops.
With eyes full of longing, they barter their dreams,
In a world where the surface is richer than seams.

"Here's a token of hope, a glimmer of grace,"
But it fades like the dusk, leaving only a trace.
For in this grand theater, where class is the play,
The lines are drawn deep, and the actors must stay.

So, what is the cost of this intricate dance?
Is it worth all the pain, the fleeting romance?
In the marketplace bustling, where hearts are laid
bare,
Class is a currency, yet no one seems to care.

"Dear heart, why do you ache in this strife?
In the hustle of status, where's the value of life?
For every smile traded, every tear that we shed,
In the end, we're just souls, seeking love instead."

Oh, Dear Heart! WHY?

Oh, dear heart, why do you care so much,
In a world that feels cold to a gentle touch?
When kindness is fleeting, and love seems a game,
Why do you yearn for a spark, a flame?

You watch as they rush, with eyes set on gain,
In the chaos of life, where compassion feels vain.
Yet still, you whisper of dreams yet to find,
Of connections that linger, of hearts intertwined.

"Why do you ache for a world that's so stark?
When shadows of selfishness swallow the light,
Why do you seek warmth in a heartless embrace?
When the dance of indifference fills every space?"

I see how you flutter with hope in your chest,
How you long for a kindness, a moment of rest.
But the world moves in circles, so dizzying, fast,
Where the echoes of empathy rarely hold fast.

"Dear heart, why do you chase after grace,
When the faces around you seem lost in the race?
Why do you long for a friend in the night?
When the stars above twinkle with distant light?"

Yet still, you beat on, with a rhythm so true,
In the silence of sorrow, you search for the few
Who might share your burdens, who might
understand?
That love is a journey, not just a demand.

"Why do you ache when the world turns away?

When the laughter of others feels hollow, astray?
Why do you wish to belong in this space?
When the heart of the world seems devoid of
grace?"

But perhaps, dear heart, it's your courage to feel,
That brings forth the beauty, the warmth that can
heal.
For in caring so deeply, despite all the pain,
You remind us of love, of hope that remains.

Oh, Dear Heart! For The Last Time.

Oh, dear heart, why do you long to be seen,
In a world that confuses the pure with the keen?
With curves that are vibrant, a spirit so bright,
You crave to be cherished, to bask in the light.

You dress in your colors, a canvas of pride,
Each stitch tells a story, your essence inside.
Yet whispers surround you, they twist and they
turn,
As they label your beauty, their judgments discern.

"Look at her flaunting, she's asking for more,"
They reduce you to labels, their words like a score.
But deep in your soul, you just want to express,
The beauty you hold, not a mere game of chess.

"Why can't they see me as more than a shape?
A heart full of longing, a dream to escape?
I wish to be noticed, to shine in my skin,
Yet dread the attention that feels like a sin."

You dance on the line, a delicate thread,
Between wanting to flourish and feeling misled.
For every admiring glance that ignites,
There's a voice that reminds you of perilous sights.

"Dear heart, how to balance the joy and the strife?
To show off your beauty while guarding your life?
To stand in your power, yet not be defined,
By the gaze of the world, the judgments aligned?"

You seek to be valued for all that you are,

Not just for the surface, the shine, or the scar.
With each step you take, you wish to reclaim
The narrative woven, to own your own name.

So, dance in your colors, let your spirit soar,
Embrace all your beauty, let them see more.
For you are a wonder, a force to behold,
A story of strength, a heart made of gold.

The Golden Cage

In a golden cage, I flutter and sigh,
A white bird dreaming beneath the vast sky.
They call me irresponsible, a role I embrace,
Yet when I spread my wings, they scorn my grace.

"Be wise, be careful," they whisper with care,
But when I reach for the sun, they pull back my air.
With every soft chirp, I long to be free,
Yet their chains of expectation weigh heavily on
me.

I chirp on the perch, show my colors so bright,
But they cut my feathers, afraid of my flight.
"Stay small, stay quiet," their voices insist,
Yet deep in my heart, a wild dream persists.

Oh, to soar high, to break through the seams,
To weave my own story, to chase all my dreams.
But here in this cage, though golden it gleams,
I'm trapped in their visions, lost in their schemes.

I am more than their whispers, more than their
fears,
A spirit unbroken, despite all the tears.
One day I'll gather the courage to rise,
To shatter these bars and embrace the wide skies.

Adaptation

In a world where the ground is barren and still,
I walk through the remnants, seeking to fulfill.
Each soul I encounter, a landscape anew,
With contours and edges that shape what I do.

To one, I'm a whisper, soft as the breeze,
A gentle reflection, hoping to please.
With another, I'm fire, fierce and unbound,
A tempest of passion, where chaos is found.

Each interaction a puzzle, a thread to untangle,
I weave through their worlds, navigating the
jangle.
For survival demands that I shift with the tide,
To blend with their rhythms, to wear what they
hide.

With the stoic, I'm steady, a pillar of calm,
An anchor in storms, a soothing balm.
Yet with the restless, I'm wild, uncontained,
A force of ambition, where dreams are unchained.

In the eyes of the hopeful, I'm a beacon of zeal,
A spark of connection, a promise to heal.
But with the wary, I'm cautious and still,
A careful observer, respecting their will.

This barren expanse offers little reprieve,
Yet I adapt to survive, to learn, to believe.
Each role I embrace is a means to endure,
A testament to strength, a heart that's secure.

In this desolate realm, where echoes persist,
I navigate pathways, each choice a twist.
For in every encounter, I find ways to thrive,
It is a place where spirits are not able to survive.

Illusion

In the crowd, you glide, a figure so sleek,
With charm that enchants, and words that can
speak.
You weave through the chatter, a pattern spun,
A master of whispers, where battles are won.

Your laughter rings clear, a melody sweet,
While secrets lie buried beneath polished feet.
You gather the praise, a crown on your brow,
Yet beneath the façade, I wonder just how.

With stories adorned, you paint every scene,
A canvas of virtue, where few have been seen.
Yet I glimpse the echoes of choices you've made,
In the silence between, where shadows have
played.

You smile with such ease, as if born to deceive,
Each glance a reflection of what you believe.
I watch as you flourish, envy takes hold,
For you wear the fortune, while I feel the cold.

But as I unravel your intricate game,
I find in the mirror, I share in the blame.
For the envy I harbor, the whispers I keep,
Are threads of my own, in a fabric so deep?

In the depths of my heart, I recognize well,
The duality woven where secrets can dwell.
For you are the image of choices I've known,
A reflection of me, in a world overgrown.

So here in this moment, I face what is true,
The person I envy, is hauntingly you.
With each step I take, I embrace what I've spun,
For the two-faced illusion is merely one.

This Dystopian World

In the cradle of youth, laughter echoes like chains,
With dreams in their eyes, yet bound by unseen
reins.
They run through the fields, but whispers invade,
"Follow the path, let your spirit be frayed."

For every giggle hides a question profound,
"Is this joy a façade, in a silence unbound?"

As they grow older, the weight starts to press,
Responsibilities rise, a relentless caress.
They toil for their families, in factories of dread,
Building futures on hopes that are already dead.

Yet beneath every smile, a secret takes hold,
"Are they truly alive, or just stories retold?"

In the twilight of life, wisdom feels like a curse,
Stories of triumph now echo in reverse.
They gather their harvest, but the fields lie bare,
With shadows of choices that linger in air.

Yet within every tale, a darkness does creep,
"Is this journey a prison, or a promise to keep?"

As they age and reflect, the cycle spins tight,
From cradle to grave, lost in endless night.
Each stage a reminder of paths paved in fear,
Yet beneath every joy, a silence draws near.

For every heartbeat, a truth starts to swell,
"Is this life we're living, a sentence from hell?"

In the stillness of night, when hope seems to fade,
The pulse of existence beats heavy, afraid.
They ponder the choices that led them astray,
As the cycle continues, consuming the day.

And with every turn, a dread starts to swell,
"Is this life we're trapped in, a story from hell?"

Thank you for giving this book time.

Author's Biography~

Bhavika Jain is a teen poet with a passion for literature and creativity. An avid reader, she draws inspiration from the characters that she reads in books, attempting to showcase the inter-connectedness of the character's perspectives into her own life experiences to craft relatable poetry. Her work explores a deep understanding of the complexities of identity while exploring how this global issue of having an identity crisis is the foundation of many of the conflicts in our world today.

With a unique writing style which focuses on minute details, Bhavika uses her writing as a platform to explore the struggles of everyday life and digs down to the root cause of them, inviting the readers to reflect on their own choices and experiences. Through her daring writing she hopes to remind us of all the connections of our "supposed" roles in society that has somewhat blinded us to what reality is.

For any inquiry please email:
bhavikajwrites@gmail.com

www.ingramcontent.com/pod-product-compliance
Lightning Source LLC
Chambersburg PA
CBHW031245130726
47988CB00008B/3241